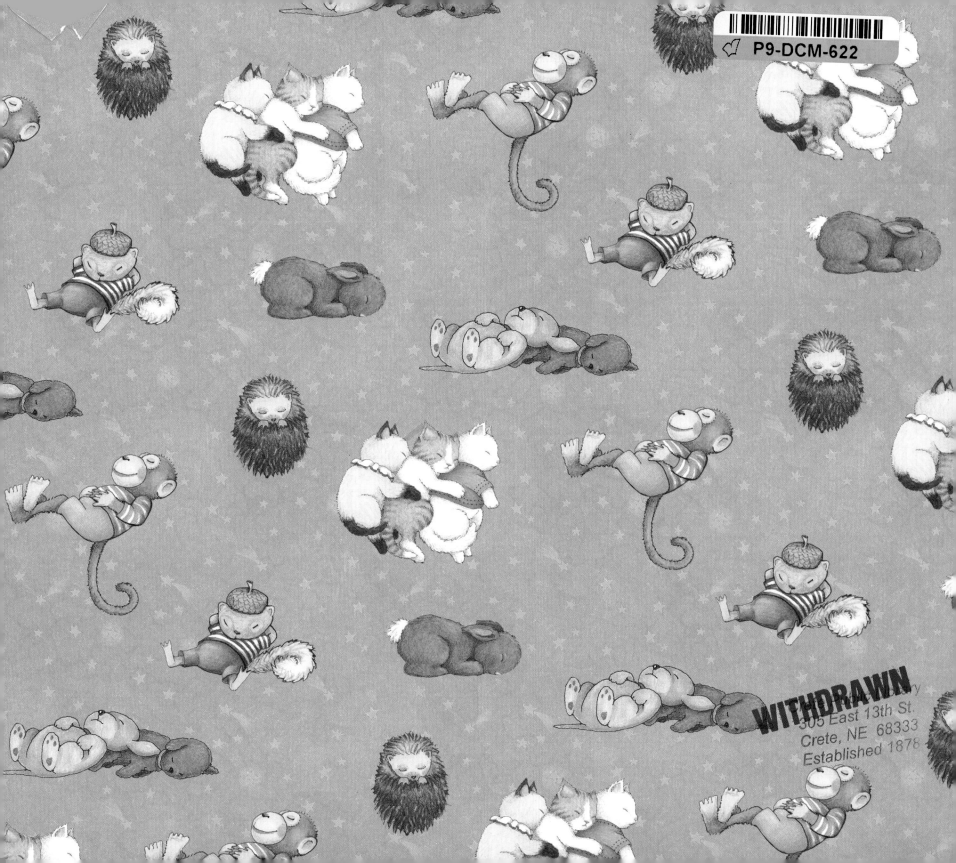

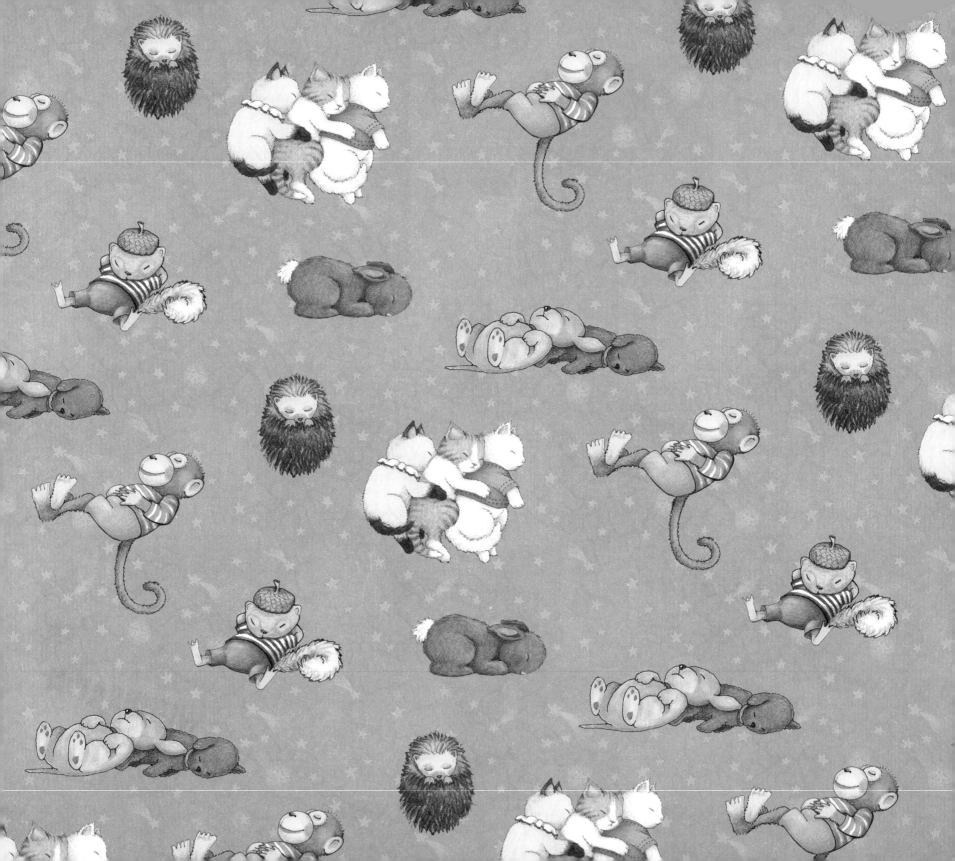

FOR

_____

FROM

_____

for
JACK & LILLY

ZONDERKIDZ

The Bedtime Book

Illustrations © 2017 by Mary Engelbreit Enterprises, Inc.
Text © 2017 Zondervan

Requests for information should be addressed to:

Zonderkidz, 3900 *Sparks Dr. SE, Grand Rapids, Michigan 49546*

ISBN 978-0-310-73329-4

Any Internet addresses (websites, blogs, etc.) and telephone numbers in this book are offered as a resource. They are not intended in any way to be or imply an endorsement by Zondervan, nor does Zondervan vouch for the content of these sites and numbers for the life of this book.

Printed in China

17 18 19 20 21 / DSC / 22 21 20 19 18 17 16 15 14 13 12 11 10 9 8 7 6 5 4 3 2 1

THE BEDTIME BOOK

MARY ENGELBREIT

ZONDER**kidz**

4

TUCKED IN TIGHT

Mama comes to tuck you in,
Pulls the covers to your chin,
Squeezes fingers, squeezes toes,
Lays a kiss upon your nose,
Checks for beasts below the bed,
Brushes stray hairs from your head,
Whispers words of love so sweet,
Helps you drift away to sleep,
Rises slowly, says good night,
Now that you are tucked in tight.

TWINKLE, TWINKLE

Twinkle, twinkle, little star,
How I wonder what you are.
Up above the world so high,
Like a diamond in the sky.

Twinkle, twinkle, little star,
How I wonder what you are.

When the blazing sun is gone,
Nothing left to shine upon.
Then you show your little light,
Twinkle, twinkle, all the night.

Twinkle, twinkle, little star,
How I wonder what you are.

Then the traveler in the dark,
Thanks you for your tiny spark;
How could he see where to go,
If you did not twinkle so.

Twinkle, twinkle, little star,
How I wonder what you are.

In the dark blue sky you keep,
Often through my curtains peep,
For you never shut your eye,
Till the sun is in the sky.

Twinkle, twinkle, little star,
How I wonder what you are.

TIME FOR BED

The day is done, it's time for bed.
"Let's go to sleep," my mama said.
She picked me up to say good night.
She wrapped me in her arms, so tight.

She set me on my comfy bed.
"Sweet dreams, my love," she softly said.
She tucked me in to say my prayers.
I heard her walking down the stairs.

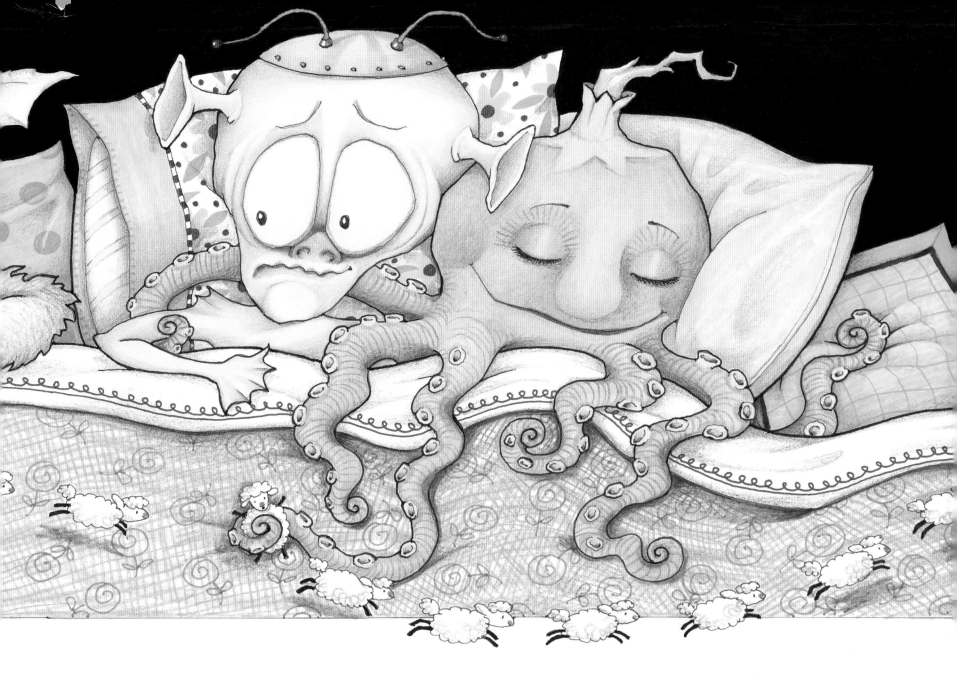

Below my bed, five monsters hid.
The lights were off and out they slid.
They climbed in bed, so quietly.
They came to say a prayer with me—

For in the dark, they are afraid.
So we all closed our eyes and prayed.
I taught the monsters to count sheep.
And then we drifted off to sleep.

SLEEPY TIME

Our God has made the twinkling stars;
He made the moon so bright,
To tell us it is sleepy time
When we can rest each night.

Our God has made the day and night
To show his love and care;
So when I play and when I sleep
I know that God is there.

MY SHEPHERD

The Lord is with me everywhere.
I'm always in my shepherd's care.
He gives me what I need each day,
He lights my path and guides my way.
He gives me rest and keeps me strong
And tells my heart what's right and wrong.
When it is dark and I can't see,
His outstretched arms will comfort me.

SOUND ASLEEP

Puppies piled high, sound asleep ...

Chicks by mama, not a peep.

Bunnies snuggled in their hutch ...

Purring kittens all must touch.

Pretty ponies in their stall ...

Hedgehogs curled up in a ball.

Baby squirrels snug in their nest ...

Swinging monkeys now at rest.

HAPPY HEARTS

We thank you, Lord, for happy hearts,
For rain and sunny weather.
We thank you, Lord, for family,
And that we are together.

THANK YOU!

Thank you for the world so sweet.
Thank you for the food we eat.
Thank you for the birds that sing.
Thank you, God, for everything.

COUNTING SHEEP

It's time for bed, but I can't sleep.
I guess I should try counting sheep.
But sheep make noise—they baaaa and bleeat.
And wool feels itchy on my feet!

A good night's sleep is what I wish.
I guess I'll just try counting fish.
Blub, blub, blub, the fish swim by,
splashing water in my eye!

I'm tired and wet and need my ZZZZs,
I guess I'll count some bumblebees.
As they fly pollen to and fro—
Their buzzing sound has got to go!

I'd like to sleep just like a log.
I guess I'll try and count some dogs.
But I forgot, they make me sneeze!
And worse than that, I now have fleas.

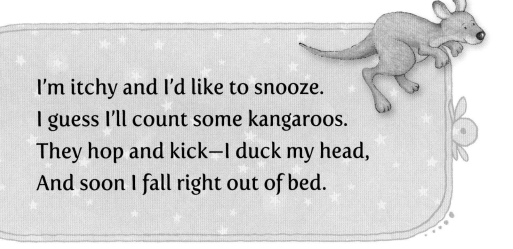

I'm itchy and I'd like to snooze.
I guess I'll count some kangaroos.
They hop and kick—I duck my head,
And soon I fall right out of bed.

Now I'm tired and really sore.
I guess I'll count some dinosaurs.
STOMP, STOMP, CRASH and BANG, BANG, BOOM—
Those creatures just destroyed my room!
Now there's a draft and it's too cold.
This counting thing is getting old.

I need some sleep—I need it bad!
I guess I'll bunk with Mom and Dad.

23

WHAT WILL TOMORROW BRING

Goodnight, young prince; the day is done.
Your knights have gone, as has the sun.
Lay down your sword and armor too,
Until tomorrow's sky turns blue.

Tomorrow will come soon, you'll see.
Tomorrow—then who will you be?
A circus star, a queen or king?
What will tomorrow bring?

Good night, princess; it's time for sleep.
Your maids are counting fluffy sheep.
Take off your crown and princess best;
It's time to snuggle down for rest.

Tomorrow will come soon, you'll see.
Tomorrow—then who will you be?
A circus star, a queen or king?
What will tomorrow bring?

Good night, my child, and happy dreams.
I know sometimes it really seems
As if the fun has just begun
When day turns night, and fun is done.

Tomorrow will come soon, you'll see.
Tomorrow—then who will you be?
A circus star, a queen or king?
What will tomorrow bring?

A GOODNIGHT PRAYER

God, we thank you for the night,
And for the pleasant morning light;
For rest and food and loving care,
And all that makes the day so fair.
Help us do the things we should,
To be to others kind and good;
In all we do, in work or play,
To grow more loving every day.

THE MAN IN THE MOON

The man in the moon
Looked out of the moon
And this is what he said,
"Tis time that, now I'm getting up,
All children went to bed."

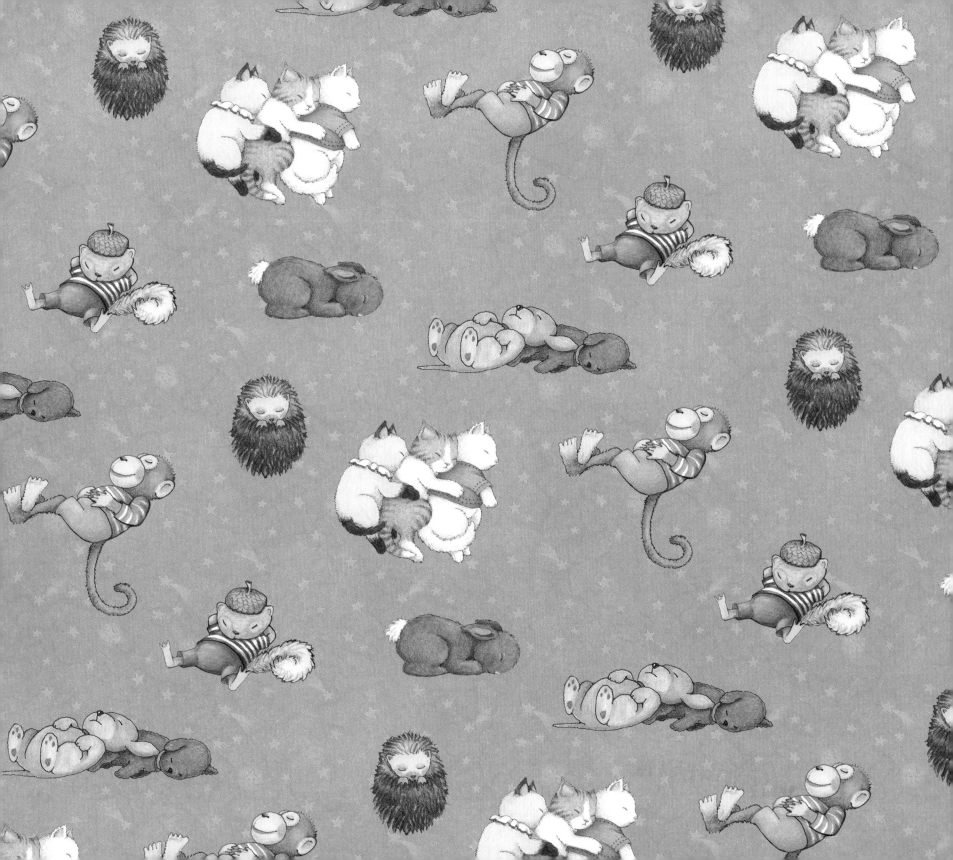